African Adventures with the Almighty's Signature

My Inspiring Stories

by Amy Hagerup

©2014 Amy Hagerup

Thank you for purchasing:

African Adventures with the Almighty's Signature:

My Inspiring Stories

ALL RIGHTS RESERVED

This book contains material protected under International and Federal Copyright Laws and Treaties. Any unauthorized reprint or use of this material is prohibited. No part of this book may be reproduced or transmitted in any form or by any means, electronic or mechanical, including photocopying, recording, or by any information storage and retrieval system without express written permission from the author / publisher.

NO DISTRIBUTION RIGHTS

You may not offer this book to anyone as a gift on your site or for monetary gain. Also, the author is not liable to be sued for any reason pertaining to this book and its stories and information. All the stories are true and are from my personal perspective and the perspective of those sited.

By downloading and/or reading these stories, you are agreeing that you are aware of these rights and disclosures and agree to everything stated here.

Table of Contents

Introduction

Chapter 1: A Foreign Country, Curfew, and Free Pepsi's

Chapter 2: When Trust Intersects with Pain

Chapter 3: Excruciating Pain in the Middle of Nowhere

Chapter 4: I Felt Like I Was Looking at Death Itself

Chapter 5: God's Provision with a Surprising Twist

Chapter 6: Volkswagon Chariot for Jesus

Chapter 7: How A Piece of Candy Caused a Problem for Isaac

Chapter 8: "Please Remove the Cup of Boarding School from Me, Lord"

Chapter 9: Two Lessons Learned from Beggars at Our Door

Chapter 10: When the Crowd Boo-ed My Son at a Track Meet

Chapter 11: A Miracle of God-Proportions at a Big Boy's Restaurant

Chapter 12: God Turns Tragedy into Music-Making

Chapter 13: And the Little Orphan Said "'Ear Esus!"

Introduction

If you receive just one message from my life and the books I write, I want it to be one of knowing how very much God loves you and cares deeply for you.

It has always been a burning desire of mine, and the purpose of my life, to help people take their next step in their journey toward God. With that in mind, I have to filter everything I do through that lens. I have to ask: "Will this help someone grow closer to the Lord and the life He has for them in following hard after Him?"

Now with limited time available to me, I have to be very laser-focused to make every effort count. I want with all my heart to maximize the impact.

And so this question precedes this collection of stories: "Will these stories truly help someone in their journey toward God?"

I knew right away that the answer was a resounding YES. And that fuels me as I write. I love to connect the dots and to see the Almighty's signature on the stories that make up my life.

As much as I delight in the writing process, I know that they are just words on a page unless they can leap from the page into someone's heart and make an impact there. I know the written word has the power to do that because I experience it myself every day. Oh, how I love to read ... and be transformed and inspired to do better.

Yes, I love writing ... but I love encouraging people even more. And that is my goal – to encourage you with the truth of how amazing God is and how He is at work in your life just as He is in mine too.

These stories are not meant to entertain you as a fiction story could accomplish that. No, these stories are shared to encourage and inspire you – to make you nod in agreement that God is indeed alive and powerful and ready to act on your behalf.

My husband and I were missionaries in Ethiopia for three years and in Ghana for twenty years. Twenty-three years, including all the furlough years in between, is a lot of time to experience God's faithfulness throughout the adventures of our lives.

As I spent time recounting these amazing short inspirational stories for my grandchildren, I decided to publish them so that others can be wowed by God's signature on our life stories. You have a story too with His signature on it. All you have to do is learn to connect the dots.

Listen now as I share some of my African adventures with the Almighty's amazing signature as only God could have done. After each one, pause and reflect on your own life as you see God's signature throughout your good times and your bad ones. He is faithful through it all.

Chapter 1: A Foreign Country, Curfew, and Free Pepsi

After we were married in Addis Ababa, Ethiopia, we had our honeymoon for two nights at the Hilton Hotel, and then for two weeks at the mission rest home in Bishoftu. After that, we had to fly to Djibouti so I could be issued my resident visa as Mrs. Mark Hagerup outside of the country.

Our plan was to fly into hot Djibouti, walk to the Ethiopian embassy, get my passport stamped with the visa, and then walk to the train station to catch the train back to Ethiopia. The train, however, only ran the route every two days.

When we landed, it felt like we were walking into an oven as we deplaned. Even the policemen had on shorts. We pawed our way through the heat to reach the embassy by noon but, alas, they had closed for the mid-day siesta ... for four hours!

The shade of a bridge provided us a bit of reprieve from the heat as we waited. Those four hours crept by for us, like children waiting for Christmas morning to get here. Finally, we gathered up our few belongings and made our way back to the embassy. Unfortunately, other desperate souls had beat us there. We edged our way into the crowd at the big irongate, and Mark stretched out his long white arm which held my passport, hoping the official there would take mine for that needed visa stamp.

After granting visas to some of the ones at the gate, they announced they would be closing until next day. Mark immediately begged for mercy in Amharic, the Ethiopian main language, while I prayed, and sure enough, the guard reluctantly took my passport. Thank you, God.

Ironically, it took only a few minutes for them to process it and the passport was back in our possession. We gratefully accepted it, giving our profuse thanks as we turned and began sprinting toward the train station. It was almost 6 PM and the train was scheduled to leave at seven! Time was of the essence. This train only travelled the route to Ethiopia every second day. If we missed the train, we were stuck in Djibouti for 48 more hours.

To complicate matters, there was a curfew in the city at 6 PM due to the local fighting, so we had to hurry. The train was in sight when we were horrified to see it begin to move and we weren't there yet! It was leaving an hour early due to the curfew. My heart sank as I realized we would be stuck in Djibouti for two days and the curfew time was on us too.

With slumped shoulders and a feeling of "what are we going to do now," we came upon a Catholic school. With brave faces that neither of us were really feeling, we tiptoed up to a big massive carved door and knocked. The priest who answered the door couldn't understand our English as we tried to ask for refuge for the night. Since Djibouti is French-speaking, it was hard to find someone who could speak English and interpret for us. Finally, a beautiful Ethiopian woman seemingly on her way home from work passed by and heard our efforts to communicate in English and gestures. Being an English speaker herself, she interpreted for us. Little did we know that she was our angel in disguise.

At first, the priest was annoyed with us and said, "I know kids like you - you say you want to stay for the night and then you stay for a month!" Remember, we were only 24 and 21 years old – and no doubt looked like we were teenagers.

We had brought enough money along in the event we had to stay in a hotel, so cash was not the problem. It was because of the curfew that we didn't have time to get to a hotel and so we needed rescuing. The priest was escorting us to the gate while shaking his head in refusal to put us up, but I think God used my tears to soften his heart. Stopping in his tracks, he motioned for us to follow him and he reluctantly led us to a small classroom. The Ethiopian woman was horrified, but we were totally satisfied – we would be safe from the rain, bugs, and the police.

We could curl up together on the floor and wait for daylight to seek out a hotel. Marta, our angel, insisted the room wasn't good – where would we wash? where would we sleep? She said, "You can come stay at my house." We tried to refuse, but she insisted that we follow her quickly.

As the street became enveloped with darkness, we followed her quick steps. We didn't know if we were going to a mud hut or a mansion - we were just trusting and following and very, very grateful.

The thirst I felt was like I had never experienced. My throat was parched, but all I knew was that we were being led to safety and hopefully, a cup of water (okay, make that a gallon of water!)

As it turned out, Marta was married to an Italian who was the owner of a Pepsi factory in Djibouti. They lived in a spacious house with their four children. Mark and I collapsed on the sofa, content to be safely off the streets, while they brought us Pepsi after Pepsi. I think we both drank four or five!

We insisted that we weren't hungry – how could we take advantage of their hospitality to give us lodging by accepting food too? But when they served supper, they invited us to join them. Oh my – we were so hungry. They served us spaghetti and it was the best ever. Remember, George was Italian.

I was so hungry that I had two big helpings not realizing that the spaghetti was the appetizer. They then served us steak!

George and Marta moved into their kids' bedrooms and gave us their bedroom. Do you see what happened here? The owner of Pepsi in Djibouti gave his bedroom up to two total strangers off the street! We were in awe.

Djibouti is so hot that water straight from the tap is scalding hot. So a person has to draw their bathwater in the morning so that by evening, it will have cooled off enough to bathe in. Marta gave me her cooled down bathwater!

She gave me a nightgown to wear, but the head opening was too small to fit over my head. But that wasn't a problem to Marta. She took the gown from me and ripped the opening to make more room for my head to fit through. These strangers were really taking care of us.

The next morning, we told them we could find a hotel for our second night even though they said we could stay with them again. We didn't want to take advantage of their kindness to us as strangers.

After everyone left for school and work, we went out and found a French Bible to buy for them. We came back and left the Bible for them with a note of thanks on the table.

Satisfied that we had thanked them well, we hailed a taxi to go to town where we found a little hotel and checked in. It was about 12:30 by now as we checked out our small, but clean room.

It seems we had just set our bags down when we heard a loud knock on our door. It was Marta with the hotel manager. She had come home from lunch and found our note, so she came looking for us in the local hotels. "You must come back to our home. It will be better for you," she sternly told us as if she were a mother hen.

Marta demanded that the manager give us our passports back since we didn't use anything, and then she paid a taxi to take us back to her house. We watched the scenery speed by as we were whisked right back to their home.

And so we spent our second night with George and Marta again. The Lord says in Matthew 6:33 "But seek first his kingdom and his righteousness, and all these things will be given to you as well." (NIV)

We truly experienced the fulfillment of this verse in Djibouti. We were there because we wanted to be missionaries in Ethiopia - we were seeking God's kingdom first.

God Almighty provided for us in Djibouti through George and Marta a second night. Same abundant food. Same nightgown torn to fit me. Same God with His signature on our plight – taking care of us as only He can.

Chapter 2: When Trust Intersects with Pain

Oftentimes, lessons on trust happen all around us – if we will just stop and listen.

During our time in Ethiopia, we lived in a village in the mountains called Waka. Waka was only accessible by small airplane or a two day mule ride/walk.

While we were there, there was political unrest in the country and the small mission airplanes that flew us in and out of Waka were temporarily grounded.

As our money and food supplies dwindled, we knew we would have to go the two day mule trek to Soddu to get more supplies.

We packed up our food and water needed for the two day trek through the mountains and got all the mules loaded up. Some of our Ethiopian friends would travel with us.

Our son was nine months old at the time so we had the added challenge of traveling with a baby on the trip.

I must say that walking through those mountains was simply breath-taking. As I rounded every bend in the path, I was overwhelmed with the beauty of God's creation all around me.

There was not a piece of litter nor a big billboard demanding our attention anywhere. Just God's beautiful handiwork.

We alternated between walking and riding the mules all day for that first day. Being in the hot sun made us more grateful than ever before for the shade of sprawling trees along the path.

It was a walk to remember for sure.

We spent the night in a village church which was a large mud hut. I had baby Benjy curled up beside me on my sleeping bag on the hard, dirt floor – quite a departure from a portable crib that I would have liked to have traveled with for my baby.

Around 1 a.m. our hostesses gently touched our shoulders to awaken us for a wonderful meal of *injerra bu whut* – the Ethiopian national food. The hospitality of Africans is amazing. Of course, they hadn't known we were coming, so they had to kill a chicken, make a fire, and prepare all the trimmings for several hours after we had arrived – and had gone to bed.

That meal tasted very, very good to these weary travelers. With full tummies, we fell back to sleep.

We awakened with the sun and rolled up our sleeping bags. The mules were very cooperative as we got them packed up again for the final leg of our trip. It would be shorter today since we planned the bulk of our journey for the first day.

After an hour had passed, I could tell that our water supply was going down faster than we had planned for.

We had about four more hours to walk before we reached the car road where some missionaries would pick us up to take us the rest of the way to the mission. We had to make the water last till we got to the pick-up point.

I remember it like it was yesterday. We were all thirsty so we got the water out.

I put the water in a cup to give my baby and he eagerly reached for it – his lips dry and cracking from being parched. I knew he was very thirsty – as I was too!

I gave him a good drink being careful not to spill a drop of the precious fluid. He drained the cup and then patted the jug, indicating that he wanted more.

I had to tell him he couldn't have more yet. I get choked up just writing this.

It was a huge lesson on trust.

To deny your thirsty baby water because you know you have to conserve it for later pierces a mother's heart like you wouldn't believe.

His pleading eyes and drooping lips begged me to give him what he wanted.

I had to withhold it for his good – so he could have a drink in another hour when the sun was even hotter. He had to trust me.

Don't you wonder if God feels like that sometimes? Needing to say no to our request because He knows the future and what we will need then?

Sometimes trust intersects with pain.

Benjy had to trust me and my unconditional love for him and what would be best for his future (albeit, a very soon future!)

And we have to trust God who loves us so very much.

"Trust in the Lord with all your heart, and lean not on your own understanding. In all your ways acknowledge Him, and He will make your paths straight." Proverbs 3: 5, 6 (NIV)

When trust intersects with pain, lean hard on the One Who sees the end from the beginning – and everything in between. You are in safe hands.

The water held out. We drained every drop with just 20 minutes left to walk. Soon we saw the land-rover with our friends waving enthusiastically to us on the other side of the torn up bridge we had to carefully cross. The planks on the bridge had been stolen – to be used for firewood – making the bridge unpassable by a vehicle. It was even precarious for us to walk over – stretching between the strong iron frame to reach the next bar safely, but that was the least of our worries.

We had made it. The Almighty brought us safely to our destination and all we had suffered was a little bit of uncomfortable thirst.

I am so thankful that I never have to thirst spiritually because I am drinking from the Living Water of Jesus.

Chapter 3: Excruciating Pain in the Middle of Nowhere

We stayed in Soddu about a week and the planes were still grounded, so we planned the two day trek walk back into our station at Waka. We had a missionary drive us to the bridge where we would start walking.

Our faithful Ethiopian friends met us on the other side of the bridge with the mules ready to receive us for the trip back into Waka.

We spent the night again in the welcoming village church and got up with the sun to begin our walk early, so we could stop during the heat of the day.

My mule seemed edgy that morning. I strapped 9 month old Benjy to me with my cloth baby carrier with him sitting in front of me on the saddle. Then I could hold him with one hand so he wouldn't bounce about so much, while I held on with my right hand.

When we were coming down a hill to a dried-up riverbed, a herd of cattle was coming from the other direction toward us. Just as we met the first cow, my mule got spooked so he spun around to head back up the hill, slinging the saddle and its clinging occupants over the side of its belly. I tensed up to protect little Benjy from the fall as we landed on a big rock. The small of my back took the brunt of the fall as I cradled Benjy like a protective mother bear, trying to keep him from getting hurt.

Benjy started crying, but he stopped as soon as his daddy took him from me. He was only scared, not injured. It was a different story for me though - I was in excruciating pain. I was sure I had broken my back and I wondered if I would ever walk again. All the Ethiopians traveling with us gathered around me and were crying "way-nee, way-nee, way-nee" which is an Ethiopian expression of distress.

Mark tried to help me to my feet but I screamed out in pain. So then all my protectors grabbed a sleeping bag off one of the mules and tried to stuff it around me to give me a bit of a cushion as I lay immoveable on the big rock. We all prayed for God to heal me and to give us wisdom whether to proceed into Waka or to return to Soddu where there was a mission hospital. My husband decided they would try again in 30 minutes to see if I could stand. During those 30 minutes, I looked into the sky and wondered how long I would lie there and would a helicopter have to be sent in to rescue me.

I wondered if I would walk again.

I wondered if my missionary career would be ended.

I wondered if I would ever have another child ... or be able to care for Benjy for that matter.

I wondered how God could use this crisis for His good.

The time clicked away as we know it always does and it was soon time to try again to see if I could get up. Mark prayed again for God's healing touch.

He gingerly grabbed my two hands as everyone watching held their collective breath.

This time I could stand! I believe the Almighty had healed me. I gingerly took one step and then two steps. I could walk! Praise God! I could walk again!

Daweet got me a strong branch to use as a walking stick and we decided to go on into Waka rather than heading back to Soddu.

Very slowly we made our way through the mountains with Mark carrying Benjy now. We sent Gulu ahead to tell our coworker in Waka who was a nurse, of my accident, and to return to meet us with jackets. Our trip now would extend into the night when temperatures would drop. In the middle of the day I began suffering from a heat stroke so we stopped to rest for several hours in the hut of a caring Ethiopian who generously brought us ripe bananas to eat.

Gulu's swift feet got the word to Cathy and then returned to us with warm jackets and a thermos of hot tea warming our insides physically as well as our hearts emotionally. We offered the tea to our fellow travelers but they refused to take any for themselves. I am continually amazed at the honor and respect Africans bestow on missionaries so generously. It is very humbling for they are so deserving of honor and respect themselves.

As we arrived, Cathy welcomed us with a standby set up on our two way radio with a mission doctor at Soddu. He questioned me and then gave instructions for me not to lift Benjy, to elevate my legs, and to wrap my legs in ace bandages. He would talk with me again daily for a few days to be sure I was okay.

Amazingly I had no recurring back pain! Once the soreness healed, I was totally fine. God had truly healed me. When I get to heaven I will ask Him if my back had been broken and He healed it.

Once I was able to walk again on that mountain path, I began to thank God. First, I thanked Him for my feet, my legs, and my back that worked. How recently had I thanked Him for the gift of walking? Then I thanked Him for my eyes that I can see, my ears that I can hear, my mouth that I can talk and eat! I thanked Him for my hands that I can touch, write, create, and hug! How wonderful is that!

You never know what all you have been blessed with until it is taken away. Our lives can change in an instant.

First Thessalonians 5:18 says "In everything give thanks, for this is God's will for you in Christ Jesus!" (NASV)

Just another amazing adventure with the Almighty's signature on it.

Chapter 4: I Felt Like I Was Looking at Death Itself

When we lived in Ghana, one of our friends told us that his wife was wasting away due to an illness that had taken over her body. He asked us to come and see her to pray for her. When I entered the dark hut and my eyes adjusted, I could see Akosua on her cot – she looked like a skeleton with skin on.

Her big, hollow eyes stared at me and I felt like I was looking at death itself. My heart went out to her in her weakened state. Tears quickly welled up in my eyes and I got choked up. Surely Akosua would be in the Lord's presence soon.

Akosua most likely had had a stroke – I don't know. All I knew was that she needed help – but what did I have to give?

I inwardly prayed for wisdom and then told her sisters and husband to bring her out into the sun every day for 30 minutes or so and to move her arms and legs each day very gently. Even to my untrained medical eye, I could see that her muscles were atrophying from disuse.

I prayed for God to have mercy on her and bring her back to health as only He can.

A few weeks later, I went to visit again. I nervously approached the circle of huts, afraid of the news I might hear when I got there. But, praise God, she was still alive.

I knelt beside her and reached out to hold her hand. Her sister told me that Akosua's little 3 year old boy would come and pray over Akosua. All he would say would be: "Dear Jesus. Amen. Dear Jesus. Amen." It was a great example of the Holy Spirit interceding for us when we don't know what to pray. This little one knew Whom to go to – he just didn't know what to say!

As Akosua laid there on her cot, I asked her caretakers how it was going with the things I had recommended.

They said they were taking her into the sun each day and that they were moving her arms and legs like I had advised.

I asked them if moving her arms and legs was hurting her and they replied: "Oh yes, she screams." Scared me to death! I quickly back pedaled and said, "Remember to be gentle. Progress slowly."

They did tell me, though, that she seemed to like being out in the sun. The warmth of the sun is a delightful gift to us as the Lord pours on the Vitamin D too!

I prayed again before I left, all the while thanking God again for the gift of health that we so often take for granted.

This made me think of the healing power of the sun that God has put into this great creation.

Soon after my second visit to Akosua, we left for furlough for a year. When we returned, I went to visit her, praying that she was still alive.

When I got to the village, I saw a happy sight: Akosua was sitting outside and she was fat! I mean she really had some good bulk on her and best of all, she had a huge smile on her face!

She was praising God for healing her.

What an amazing God we have! From literally skin and bones being right at death's doorstep, Akosua was healed and now had the joy of the Lord on her face.

Jeremiah 17:14 says "Heal me, O Lord, and I will be healed; Save me and I will be saved, for Thou art my praise." (NASV)

The Almighty is definitely Jehovah Rapha – Our Healer!

Chapter 5: God's Provision with a Surprising Twist

I've always loved things that matched.

I would sew matching outfits for my preschoolers.

Organizing my cupboards with matching containers was fun for me.

When we had our first baby and lived in a remote village in Ethiopia, I used red gingham cloth to make curtains for the windows and a skirt to put around a big barrel to use for the changing table. Then I used red material to cover pieces of cardboard to make mats for some cute teddy bear photos I got from an old calendar to hang on the wall. As rustic and homemade as it was, my baby's room matched and I loved it.

It was one of the quirks God put in me: I like matching things.

That leads me to a story of God's provision with a surprising twist.

When we were packing up for our first four year missionary term in Ghana, it was a daunting task to buy everything we needed to set up our household there with two children and another one on the way. I made a chart of each child with how old they would be on each birthday and Christmas for the four years we would be there so I could take presents for them for each event.

And the funny thing was - we didn't even know if our third child who would be born after we got there was a boy or a girl. So I had to plan for gifts that were gender neutral. (She is a girl, by the way.)

For the kitchen, I purchased a 2 quart and a 3 quart saucepan, a frying pan, and a pressure cooker. I figured that would be enough for my cooking needs.

However, once we got there, I was frustrated that I hadn't brought along a smaller saucepan. My smallest pan was 2 quarts, so it was now difficult to make a small amount of oatmeal or to boil a few eggs.

To be honest, I don't even remember praying about it - I can't remember asking God to provide me with some smaller saucepans. I would just make do.

Did God even care about such a small problem anyway when there were people dying of hunger? After all, they need food - not a smaller saucepan!

About a month later, we made a trip to Accra and visited some missionary friends there that we knew from our church back in Illinois. As we chatted, I told Donna about my dilemma in not bringing any small saucepans.

Donna's eyes lit up and she said, "Oh, Amy, I have two extra small saucepans that I never use. They are just pushed back in the back of the cabinet. You can have them!"

I followed her into the kitchen like an eager puppy dog about to get a treat. I never knew I could get so excited anticipating the gift of two small saucepans.

She pulled out her frequently used pots and set them on the floor. Then she reached way back into the back of the cupboard and pulled out a 1 quart and a 1 and 1/2 quart saucepan along with their lids.

As soon as they came into my view, I gasped. I couldn't believe what I was seeing.

The pots that she was giving me matched my other two bigger saucepans! They were from the same set!

God's provision is sometimes surprising.

God is such an amazing gift-giver. He delights in giving us good gifts. He loves to see His children delighted.

Was it important that these two pots matched my set?

Of course not!

But God knew that I would like that. So in His sovereignty, whoever gave these pots to my friend or when she bought them, He had them be the same ones that would match my set because He was planning to get them to me - His precious daughter whom He knew loved for things to match.

As I thanked my friend profusely, she calmly said as she gave me a hug: "They were meant for you all along, Amy."

Don't ever underestimate God's provision earmarked for you.

Don't ever put God in a box of how you think He will provide for you.

God is a wonderful Father Who loves to delight His children.

Matthew 7:11 says "If you, then, though you are evil, know how to give good gifts to your children, how much more will your Father in heaven give good gifts to those who ask him!" (NIV)

Just like you enjoy surprising your children with good gifts, God loves to surprise you too. Ask God for what you need this week and then watch for a surprise provision from Him.

Chapter 6: Volkswagon Chariot for Jesus

This story doesn't take place in Africa, but it is during our furlough from Africa. Since God is not geographically limited, it makes total sense that He continues His amazing adventures in other places we find ourselves!

When we were on furlough in 1982, Mark's parents in Illinois provided us with a small car for our transport needs for the year. Don't you love how God's provision can be channeled through His children?

When we were ready to return to Ghana, we flew from Illinois to South Carolina to be with my family for two weeks before the flights over the ocean. We needed a car to get us around to those last minute doctor appointments and shopping trips, so we asked our church family at August Street Church if anyone had a car to loan us for two weeks.

One couple, Rob and Barri Sweet, responded that they had just purchased a new volkswagon van and were still in possession of their old van which they planned to sell. They explained to us that they would just hang onto the old van for a couple more weeks so they could loan us a vehicle to use.

What a great provision! We were very grateful!

That afternoon they drove both vans over to my mom's home where we were staying. We chatted casually in the yard and then Rob handed my husband the keys to the NEW van!

I tried to refuse the keys to the new van and said, "Oh no, Rob. We don't want to use your new van! We just want to use the old one to get around town these last two weeks."

Rob didn't miss a beat though.

He looked at me with a surprise look on his face. "Amy, we are not giving the van to YOU. We are giving it to Jesus. And we want to give Him our BEST!"

Wow! What a testimony. I want to give Jesus my best too.

That got me to thinking.

Do I give Jesus the best time of my day?

Do I give Him the best of my spiritual gifts?

Do I give Him the best part of my paycheck?

Do I give Him my best attention to His Word?

Or do I give Jesus second best ... or even the dregs of my active life?

Mark 12:41-44 tells us of the poor widow who put two small copper coins into the treasury. Jesus told his disciples that she put in more than all the other contributors because the others put in out of their surplus, but she, out of her poverty, put in all she had to live on.

She gave her best ... all of it!

God's beautiful signature on her life ... and I'm sure He provided everything she needed.

How about you?

Do you give Jesus your best?

Chapter 7: How A Piece of Candy Caused a Problem for Isaac

Here is a fun lesson from one of my adventures in Ghana. It is not some amazing intervention from the Almighty but it is a sweet, sweet story that God used to grow my heart. Know what I mean?

During our time in beautiful Ghana in West Africa, we lived for 11 years in Kumasi, and then moved further north in Tamale for about 9 years.

While we were in Kumasi, I would visit ladies in a village called Apromase to teach Bible Studies with all my friends there. One of my friends had a baby named Isaac.

When I would go into the village, I would carry Isaac on my back with a cloth as was the custom there. Over a few years, Isaac grew to know me and love his rides on my back when I went visiting in the village. I think he might have thought of me as his white Momma.

After moving to Tamale, I didn't see Isaac for a few years. During one of our trips south, we decided to stop in Apromase and greet all our friends there. Part of our hearts were still there in that special village. I knew I would see Isaac so I took a piece of hard candy in my pocket to give him.

As we walked along the dirt road, I breathed in the dusty air and embraced with my heart the depth of friendships I had in this village. Women came running out of their huts to greet me and we chattered away as if time had stood still since my last visit.

Then I saw him - a handsome boy about 6 years old approaching me hesitantly - almost like he was wondering if it was really his long lost white mama. I knew it had to be Isaac. I knelt down and embraced his black glistening body.

For a brief instant I thought of how God loves this precious child ... and every precious child like Isaac ... and I wished I could hug each of them and look into their eyes and let them know how very valuable they are!

I reached into my pocket and pulled out the small piece of hard candy I had brought along for Isaac. His eyes brightened as he eagerly accepted my gift.

Isaac was suddenly surrounded by 7 little boys, begging Isaac to share with them. My heart sank and I thought "Why didn't I bring a whole handful of candy to give out?" That would have been so easy to do!

But Isaac didn't seem particularly frustrated by his dilemma. Rather he seemed to be basking in his new-found popularity and power of being the owner of the piece of hard candy which he could do whatever he wanted with - whether to enjoy it himself or to give it to a lucky recipient.

Then something very unusual happened - something I would have never imagined in a million years.

Isaac unwrapped the candy and put it between his teeth where he crunched down on the candy, breaking it into tiny pieces. He then put the broken pieces into the palm of his hand.

Without any fanfare, he gingerly picked up one tiny piece and gave it to one of the begging boys. Then he took another piece and generously doled it out to the next pair of outstretched hands. He did this with all the pieces until they were all gone.

Big smiles were shared all around as his friends sucked on their tiny piece of sweetness on their tongues.

But the biggest smile of all was on Isaac's face. He had taken what little treat he possessed - one piece of hard candy - and shared it out with his little friends.

And that was when it hit me. My response to the "problem" was to feel bad that I hadn't brought in more candy.

Isaac's response to the "problem" was that it wasn't a problem at all - all he had to do was to divide up what he had so that everyone could share in the windfall.

I don't know about you, but I want to be more like Isaac today - generous with what I have, rather than waiting for more surplus before being generous.

That reminds me of the verse in Acts 20:35 where the Lord says "It is more blessed to give than to receive."

Truly Isaac modeled this truth to me.

Chapter 8: "Please Remove the Cup of Boarding School from Me, Lord"

While we were missionaries in Ghana, it became clear to my husband and me that our oldest 3 kids needed more input into their lives than what we could give them.

The possibility of boarding school loomed before me.

The first stages weren't that stressful – praying, researching, praying, visiting schools, praying, interviewing teachers, parents, and students, and praying some more.

The decision stage was another story. My head knew all the positives for our kids, but my heart said "NO" – I want to hang onto them! I would ask the Lord to remove the "cup" of boarding school from me – but then I would add, "but not my will, but Yours be done."

Once it was obvious that boarding school was His plan for us, I changed my prayer to "show me that this plan is good – good for us and good for our kids."

You see, my view of our lives was limited to my earthly view.

What I could see was that I wanted to be the main influence in my kids' lives – I wanted to be the one teaching them, walking beside them, tucking them into bed. But God could see everything and He knew that boarding school would be best for our family. He wanted me to trust Him.

In seeking God in prayer, we want to line up our will with His will. How often do we cry out, "Lord, I don't know how to pray about this?" Romans 8:26 – 27 says: "the Spirit also helps our weakness; for we do not know how to pray as we should, but the Spirit Himself intercedes for us ... He intercedes for the saints *according to the will of God.*"

What we are doing when we pray is that we are holding something up before the Lord Who is wiser than we are and Who desires as our Heavenly Father to give us all good things.

To "ask God" doesn't mean to beg and plead with God for something we decide that we want, but rather to seek *His will.*

I like to call Jeremiah 33:3 "God's phone number."

It says "Call to me, and I will answer you and tell you great and mighty things which you don't know."

Have you ever been trying to do something hard but you refused to ask anyone to help you?

Asking for help is a humbling thing. When you ask for help, you are admitting that you can't do something alone. God wants us to call to Him - to ask Him.

Next the Lord says "and I will answer you." Do you ever feel like God is not answering your prayers? God's will (and His answer) always agrees with His Word with no contradictions.

So God wants us to hold up our requests to the Lord and pray in the light of His promises and commands which are *His will.* Then we can watch and see Him reveal His will to us.

The last part of that verse says "and tell you great and mighty things which you do not know."

Now think about this: how would you feel if the President of the US called you to say "I want to tell you something amazing that you don't know!" You would be thrilled and honored and your heart would pound.

That is what the God of the universe has said to us: "Call to me and I will answer and tell you great and mighty things which you do not know!"

This is called a conditional promise. It is a promise where God says: "If you do this, I will do this." In this case, call to Him and He will answer and tell us great and mighty things we don't know.

I don't know about you but I want to do my part of calling! I want to rest in knowing His will is exactly what I want ... even when it is hard to follow.

So, yes, Ben, Deeanne, and Heidi all attended boarding school for more than half of their school years. They all three even graduated from the boarding school.

God used it in their lives as a part of the life He was crafting them for. He used it as an important part of their stories and their heritage. And He used it in my life too to teach and grow me. Of course, it wasn't always easy – but then everyone has difficult things in their lives.

Boarding school was definitely an adventure for our family with God's signature on it.

Praise God for helping me to say yes to His perfect will for our family and then blessing us as a result of that.

Chapter 9: Two Lessons Learned from Beggars at Our Door

When we returned to Ghana after a four month furlough in August 1985, there was a famine going on. Food was scarce and many of our Ghanaian friends had visibly lost weight.

We didn't want to buy food on the side of the road because we knew that Ghanaians needed it more than we did. If they didn't sell it (bananas, oranges, or whatever), they would eat it themselves.

Our own supply of food was low, but we could travel to the neighboring country of Togo to get food supplies – which would happen in a couple of weeks.

One evening an old married couple came to our back door begging for food. The man seemed weaker than the woman. My heart ached for them as I went to examine my mostly-empty pantry.

I pushed aside the bottles of ketchup and vinegar, looking for what could actually be consumed as a meal. The only things I had were four small cans of mackerel, about a 2 pound bag of rice, and some eggs that were in the refrigerator. I decided to give half of everything we had while asking the Lord to supply the food I would need to feed my family until we could make the trip to Togo to buy more food.

Two Lessons Learned from Beggars at Our Door

Okay. I need to add a disclaimer here. Don't think that I was always so magnanimous because I wasn't. I'm sure there were many, many times when I could have been more generous than I was, or at least, have a more cheerful spirit giving than I did. But I don't really like to share about those times!

Benjy, who was nine years old at the time, had witnessed all of this and his heart of compassion went out to the elderly couple too. He ran to his bedroom and grabbed some of his cedis (Ghanaian currency) for me to add to the food and money I was giving them.

After I shared the provisions with them, I sat on the step beside them and told them I had something much better to offer them than these few items. I told them about the Living Bread and how Jesus loves them and had died for their sins.

I shared Romans 3:23 where it says that we are all sinners and fall short of God's grace. And then Romans 6:23 that says the wages of our sin is death, but the gift of God is eternal life through Jesus Christ our Lord. John 1:12 made it all clear to them: "But as many as received Christ, to them He gave the power to become the sons of God, even to those who believe on His name."

I was trying to communicate to them in my rusty Twi, but I believe the Holy Spirit filled in the gaps and they accepted the Lord Jesus into their lives that night.

The joy I felt of a new sister and brother in the Lord far outweighed my wondering how our family would get enough food over the next week.

As we know, God is never late. He has a perfect record as a Provider. And yet we still will sometimes say with our hearts, "Lord, I know you have a perfect record of providing for us. But I just have one question: what about tomorrow?" We chuckle as we realize the absurdity of this and yet it is true, isn't it? Aren't we like that?

The next day some missionary friends, the Hansens, came over with a basket of food. They said, "We know you haven't been able to get to Togo yet so we brought some food to help you out."

Wow – the Almighty's signature already!

Where we lived in Ghana made our home a good stopping point for missionaries travelling between the north and the south. It so happened that the same day that the Hansens brought that basket of food by, a fellow missionary, Mark Lundstedt, stopped by to overnight with us on his way to Accra.

And guess what? Yes! He brought us food too: a half a sack of powdered milk. His words were: "I know you are just back from furlough and haven't been able to go to Togo yet, so Tedde and I thought we would share our milk powder with you!"

Wow! Our pantry was getting fuller and fuller!

But God wasn't done yet. He was pulling out all the stops!

The next day a young missionary couple with the Southern Baptist mission stopped by our home. They carried in two grocery bags with them. Inside the bags were canned food items from America including a ham! (Are you laughing yet?)

Even the brown grocery bags were from an American grocery store! Doesn't God have a sense of humor?

They said, "We are cleaning out our pantry before we leave on furlough and we thought maybe you could use some foodstuffs since you haven't been able to go to Togo yet!"

God certainly was providing all of our needs according to his riches in glory ... even a ham from America! Thank You, Jesus.

About a week later, we arrived home one evening to find this dear elderly woman on our back step again with her head bowed and her hands covering her face. She seemed to be crying.

I got out of the car and went to sit beside her. My stomach twisted into a knot as I felt her sadness and knew right away the cause of it. Her loving husband had died.

I held her for a while, just letting my embrace and tears communicate to her spirit that I hurt with her. I then shared with her the hope of glory and the joy of knowing her husband was out of misery and with the living God. I John 5:13 says, "These things I have written to you who believe in the name of the Son of God, so that you may know that you have eternal life."

Her smile and nod told me that she understood. We would see him again some day.

So I actually learned two lessons from these beggars who came to my door.

First of all, I learned that the most important thing to share with people is spiritual food that can give eternal life. Always be ready in season and out of season to share about God with others. (II Timothy 4:2) Life is short and we never know when it might be someone's last chance to hear before they enter eternity!

Second of all, I learned again how we can't out-give God. I shared when I didn't know how I would feed my family until we were able to travel to Togo, but God abundantly showered provisions on us from many different sources. Philippians 4:19 says, "And my God will supply all your needs according to His riches in glory in Christ Jesus." (NASB)

I was so very thankful that I had obeyed the Lord's prompting to share with them our physical food and more importantly, sharing the spiritual food that could give life eternal.

It was as if my burgeoning pantry had a tag on it that said, "With love, from God."

Chapter 10: When the Crowd Boo-ed My Son at a Track Meet

Ever since Ben was little, he would run with his dad. Once he reached middle school age, Mark and Ben would enjoy a brisk cup of coffee before dawn, and then trek out to the stadium two miles from our home in Kumasi. Ben would peel off his shoes and socks and run for a mile while his dad ran 3 miles.

During Ben's junior year at boarding school, his P.E. teacher announced the forming of a team for track and field which would compete with other African schools. Quite a few of the guys joined for the short sprints and different field events, but no one volunteered to compete in the long distance runs.

Most of the students came from families of American missionaries and they knew they didn't stand a chance against their African counterparts. Most African guys walked miles to school and worked long and hard on the family farms afterwards. For "leisure" they would pour themselves into playing soccer. The pressure cooker of the average African boy's life demanded endurance for mere survival.

Despite all of this, Ben signed up to run the 3.5 kilometer race and started training.

Mid-afternoon three weeks later the track and field team arrived at the stadium. A sizeable crowd had gathered in the stands and the teams of athletes stood haphazardly on the field. Ben told me later that the butterflies in his stomach were going crazy. Several members of his team competed in their respective events which only heightened Ben's uneasiness.

He thought, "Those Africans run without running. They neither breathe hard nor slow down. And I will be running against them! What was I thinking?"

Finally, the participants in Ben's race were called to the track. He was the only white among 39 African guys. Their supple, powerful brown legs and arms mirrored hard work and training. Ben wondered what would become of him in this unequal race.

Here is Ben's account of what happened:

"The gun shot broke into my frenzied thoughts. Forty pairs of legs started running: one pair white, the rest black. After the initial fast start from giddiness, I forced myself into a more realistic pace and focused on my breathing. My African opponents, however, never slowed down. That initial fast start became their normal pace. I could not believe it!

Everyone else passed me in less than half a minute, leaving me the caboose of the race. The crowds in the stands stood up and booed at me. 'Look at that white boy trying to run. He doesn't stand a chance ... Hey you, give up." A defiant resolution enabled me to shrug off the crowd's discouraging taunts and keep going.

Midway through the run, the first signs of fatigue – aching and heavy breathing – hammered in my mind. Though the African sun was setting, heat simmered from the track. Inhaling the dry, dusty air left my throat slightly sore. As if this were not enough, the lead runner had just "lapped" me. I wanted to dig a hole right there in the middle of the track.

But I was determined to keep going. I maintained my pace and started gaining on some runners. When I passed them, they would dive into the unorganized group of athletes watching on the field and tear off their number which identified them, giving up in shame. After passing two or three runners, my goal rose from just completing the race to not coming in last, thus finishing with some honor.

The crowd's laughing had quieted down to a dull roar. I continued running and consciously reserved some energy for the home stretch.

One lap from the end, I quickened my pace. Adrenaline and an iron will kept me going even as more fatigue enveloped me. I noticed a runner 10 yards ahead of me. 'Could I possibly beat him?' I determined to try with all my might.

Before engaging the 'afterburners,' I steadily approached him from behind. I matched each of his strides with one and a half of my own and slowly reeled him in. I could hear his heavy breathing, smell his sweat, and feel his aching legs.

The time had come: I switched lanes and opened up the throttle. With heart racing and legs pumping furiously, I edged passed him. To my utter surprise, the crowd stood up and began cheering for me. The roar of applause shocked me into yet a faster pace. Without looking back, I sprinted fiercely to the finish line.

I had completed the race and endured until the end, winning a great personal victory."

Ben endured to the end – despite the naysayers … who changed their tune when they saw that Ben persevered.

Hebrews 10:36 says "For you have need of endurance, so that when you have done the will of God, you may receive what was promised." (NASB)

Be sure you focus on your goal and filter out all the naysayers around you. Remember that God is right by your side, helping you through your adventure – whatever it may be.

Chapter 11: A Miracle of God-Proportions at a Big Boy's Restaurant

n 1991 Mark and I went to Champaign-Urbana to check out the University of Illinois as a possible school for Ben to attend. Ben and the girls had returned to Africa to be there in time for their boarding school to start. Mark and I had two more months of furlough and so we were checking out U of I while visiting supporters.

While we were there Mark decided to stop by the Eisner grocery store where he used to work as stock boy. He had always wanted to share Christ with his boss, Dale Lehigh, but never got up the courage. Dale had been a wonderful boss, and Mark thought that perhaps Dale would still be working there and he could witness to him – even though this was 20 years later!

When we were checking out to pay for our apples and other things for our trip, Mark asked the salesclerk if Dale Lehigh still worked there. She said yes but that he was not in that day. The gal in line behind us heard us mention him, and she said "Oh, he is my Dad!"

So Mark asked about Dale and told her to greet her dad for him – even though her dad probably wouldn't remember him. What a "coincidence" that his daughter was in line behind us! (Definitely the Almighty's signature, wouldn't you agree?)

As we drove away, Mark continued to lament his regret that he had never shared his testimony with Mr. Lehigh – he lost the opportunity and now it was gone forever.

We traveled about 45 minutes on the highway and decided to stop for supper. We got off at an exit and looked around at the multiple choices of restaurants that there always is at any one exit. We chose Big Boy's – one of our favorites. We were seated at the front window and ordered our food – all the while with this cloud of regret still hanging over Mark.

I happened to glance out the restaurant window we were seated at and saw the car parked right there in front of us. I said to Mark, "How do you spell Lehigh?" He then spelled it out for me, and I said "You mean like that license plate right there?"

He looked in amazement out the window and sure enough, there was an Illinois license plate with "LEHIGH" written in large letters. Mark got so excited.

Could it be that Dale was right here in the restaurant with us? What were the odds of that? After all, we were about 45 miles away from Champaign-Urbana. We watched the car, waiting for the owners to come out to it. When they came, Mark shouted with joy, "That's him! Pay the bill, Amy – I can't miss this chance again!!!" He ran outside and caught Dale before he drove away.

As it turned out, Dale had accepted the Lord a few years before. His wife chided Mark and said, "You should have told him back then, but he has found the Lord now."

Mark's guilty conscience was finally assuaged. God in all his sovereignty, brought us to the same restaurant at the same time as Dale Lehigh. He had seated us at the right table so that we would see his license plate because he had caused Dale to park there in the right direction so we would see his license plate. Lots and lots of "God-incidents" to bring to pass God's perfect will for us in meeting up with Dale again.

God knew Mark's heart to be obedient and He orchestrated everything to bring those two together. His signature indeed!

Chapter 12: God Turns Tragedy into Music-Making

Back in 1992, a Dagomba woman named Sanatu gave birth to a baby girl in a mud hut in Ghana, West Africa. After giving birth, 18 year old Sanatu propped herself up on her elbows to look at her baby. A tear came down her cheek as she gazed at her tiny daughter, but then she fell back into the midwife's arms and died. All the midwives started wailing "Oh Sanatu" while leaving the newborn alone in the corner of the mud hut.

For about the next week or so, they would feed the baby girl water when she cried – just waiting for her to die. In the village there, the belief was that the baby caused the mother's death and if she was allowed to live, she would cause someone else to die.

Because of that superstition, no effort was made to save the baby's life.

Finally, a friend of the baby's uncle, Ahmedu, came into the village and saw that the family was leaving the baby to die. Ahmedu, who refused to let this child die, got permission from the family and the village chief to take her to the orphanage in town which he did on his motorcycle. It was there that she was named Zenabu because she had to have a name to be enrolled.

The orphanage matrons greeted me warmly as I came on my weekly visit to play with the babies. I had heard that there was a new baby enrolled and I wanted to meet her. My teenage kids were home from boarding school and I thought it would be awesome to bring the new baby to our home for a few days to love on her and help my teens learn how to care for a newborn. The orphanage administrators allowed and encouraged home visits for the orphans because they knew the personal attention was good for the babies.

But when I saw the tiny infant, my heart skipped a beat. She was only 4 ½ pounds at three weeks old. Her tiny, perfect body hardly made a bump in her crib. My friends at the orphanage asked me if I wanted to take her for a home visit and I quickly declined. I knew she should be in an incubator and she was probably going to die. I would be so traumatized if she died while in my care.

My heart was burning within me as I returned home. I told the family about tiny Zenabu and they all enthusiastically wanted to bring her to our home for a visit. We prayed about it and then decided to take the risk of having such a tiny baby in our care.

Zenabu stayed with us for three days and then she stayed with other missionary friends of ours for three more days.

We were seriously considering adopting Zenabu, but I knew this was a huge decision and we needed God's wisdom for making the right choice.

I happened to be reading in Deuteronomy 30 for my devotions that day and God made the answer so clear to me! The entire chapter is pretty awesome, but let me share from verses 11, 14, & 19.

He said, "For this commandment which I command you today is not too difficult for you, nor is it out of reach. But the word is very near you, in your mouth, and in your heart, that you may observe it ... I have set before you life and death ... so choose life in order that you may live, you and your descendants." (NASB)

"Choose life! You know what to do – it is already in your heart!"

It is entirely possible that Zenabu would have died if we hadn't adopted her – we don't know.

We adopted Zenabu and added Kinza to her name which means 'treasure' in Arabic. When we were deciding whether or not to adopt her, my husband said, "I feel like the man in the parable who found a treasure in a field and then sold all he had to buy the field so he could get the treasure. I believe Zenabu is that treasure!" And we actually named her Kinza before we knew that it means "treasure" in Arabic!

Kinza's birth mother's untimely death was tragic. The tiny baby not being given nourishment rips our hearts out. But God intervened and used Ahmedu to save Kinza's life. God further wove the story of her life when He led us to adopt her. He put music in her heart and it flows out of her. If she is happy or if she is sad, the music she plays reveals her heart.

It's kind of poignant to think of her birth in a mud hut, the death of her birth mother, and the resulting music that this daughter creates.

God is the One Who turns tragedy into music-making as only He can. Whatever tragedy you are experiencing right now can be turned into music by the One Who created music.

Isaiah 61:3 says that He comforts "those who mourn, giving them a garland instead of ashes, the oil of gladness instead of mourning, the mantle of praise instead of a spirit of fainting. So they will be called oaks of righteousness." (NASB)

God's loving signature is all over Kinza's life – both her physical life and her spiritual life.

Kinza came to us in a tiny 4 ½ pound bundle. The tag could have read, "to the Hagerups, with love, God."

Chapter 13: And the Little Orphan Said "'Ear Esus!"

You won't believe this but we actually got another love bundle from God – this time in a 14 lb package of a 22 month old baby girl. But I am getting ahead of myself.

On December 23rd, 1995, 22 month old Colette arrived in our home from the orphanage with the help of her social worker, Modesto, and her paternal grandfather. She had lost her young mother who was just 12 or 13 years old, when Colette was just a week old. Her sweet grandfather, Gaboy, saved her life by bringing her to the orphanage.

It didn't take long to decide to adopt Colette so we hired a well-known lawyer and were working on all the formalities. One day Mark came home from town and announced that he had bad news. He proceeded to tell me that our lawyer was now refusing to take Colette's case because the birth registrar had written on her birth certificate that she was a citizen of Burkina Faso instead of Ghana.

This put a definite dilemma on her case since we were pursuing the legalities of adopting her in Ghana. The paternal grandfather had come from Burkina as a three-year-old but had lived in Ghana the rest of his life. His son, Colette's birth father, had been born in Ghana. Our lawyer was concerned about what was on her birth certificate.

That night, my heart was breaking. I tried to put up a brave front as I put Kinza and Colette to bed. I had been teaching two-year-old Colette how to pray, but this night, I was going to ask Jesus to give her to us as I laid her down in her crib.

I began to pray out loud. "Dear Jesus." And then I heard a little voice from inside the crib saying, "ear 'Esus!" Colette thought I was prompting her to pray.

So I continued the prayer from her viewpoint. "Please give me to this family. I need a family and I want to learn about you. You can do anything. I love you. Amen."

Tears were spilling out of my eyes now. I crept outside in the darkness and pulled one of our string lawn chairs out under the mango tree. The stars were bright and I felt like I could touch them. I began to talk to my loving Heavenly Father.

"Father in heaven, the Red Sea is in front of us. This is a humanly impossible situation. The lawyer won't take the case. Only You can part the Red Sea. All we can do is to stand by and see your salvation just like the children of Israel did when they were faced by the Red Sea."

Just then it began to rain. I felt like the Lord was crying with me. It was the first rain of the rainy season too.

The Lord brought to my mind Hosea 6:3 – "Come - let us press on to know the Lord! His going forth is as certain as the dawn and He will come to us like the rain, like the spring rain watering the earth." (NASB)

I knew the Lord was going to answer me, just like He sent the rain, just like the sun would rise tomorrow. I only had to wait on Him.

A few days later our lawyer sent a message that we should come to see him. When we got there, he told us, "I've decided to take your adoption case after all. I know what I'm going to do."

We didn't know what changed his mind, but we did know Who had changed it.

On April 17, 1996 Colette Ishetu was awarded to us in the Tamale High Court. She became a Hagerup.

Nothing is too hard for the Lord.

Conclusion

These true stories reveal over and over again how our God is an awesome God. The Almighty's signature is all over my life.

He is such a great God and He wants us to take time to stop and reflect and "connect the dots" as I like to say, so we can see His amazing design on our lives.

His Almighty signature is on your life too. Whatever you have been through and whatever you are going through now, God promises that He is working out all those events for good – the happy ones and the sad ones and the "just daily everyday living ones" for those who love Him and are called according to His purposes. (from Romans 8:28 & 29)

Go gently now with the Great Shepherd,

Amy Hagerup

About Amy Hagerup

I am a writer, speaker, health advocate, Mom to 5, mother-in-love to 3, Nana to 13, and passionate about helping others in their lives. Having lived in Africa as a missionary for 23 years, worked at a liberal college campus for four years, stood alongside my husband when he pastored a church in the area of missions for five years, and now living a life of serving others while making an income - - you can imagine, I have experienced a lot of our faithful God's signature on my life stories! I am so blessed to be a child of the Almighty and He continues to bless me in every way. I want to share His blessings with you too!

At http://AmyHagerup.com, as The Vitamin Shepherd, I want to guide you to powerful health choices. Grab my free ebook called "11 Warning Signs You Must Not Ignore for Your Best Health."

At http://HealthyChoices4u.com, I write more specifically about natural health products and habit to help you be healthier.

My facebook fanpage is http://www.fb.com/yourhealthisyourwealth.

All my other social media handles are my name amyhagerup.

Let's connect there too.

Thank You, my friend!

Go gently now,

Amy Hagerup

Made in the USA
Middletown, DE
26 January 2018